Dedicated to my patrons at Patreon.com. From the bottom of my heart I say, "Thank you!" Your monthly contributions and support made this cookbook happen, and you keep me going like the lights that you all are. Thank you for being part of my life!

Dawn Bartel, Kelly Brown, DG Gothic, Linda Dick, Nena Dunn, Paul Canaday-Elliott, Roger & Debby Espinor, Michael Jude, David Harmon, Cindy Harris, Joey Herbert, Brenda Quint Gaebel, Peter Gunn & Lee-Anne Flandreau, Jeri Haskins, Greg & Angela O'Neal, Antonia Torrez, Marquita & John Kudrna, Amy Johnson, Naomi LaViolette, Nora Timm, and Todd Weedman.

SEASON ONE COOKBOOK

MARTI MENDENHALL

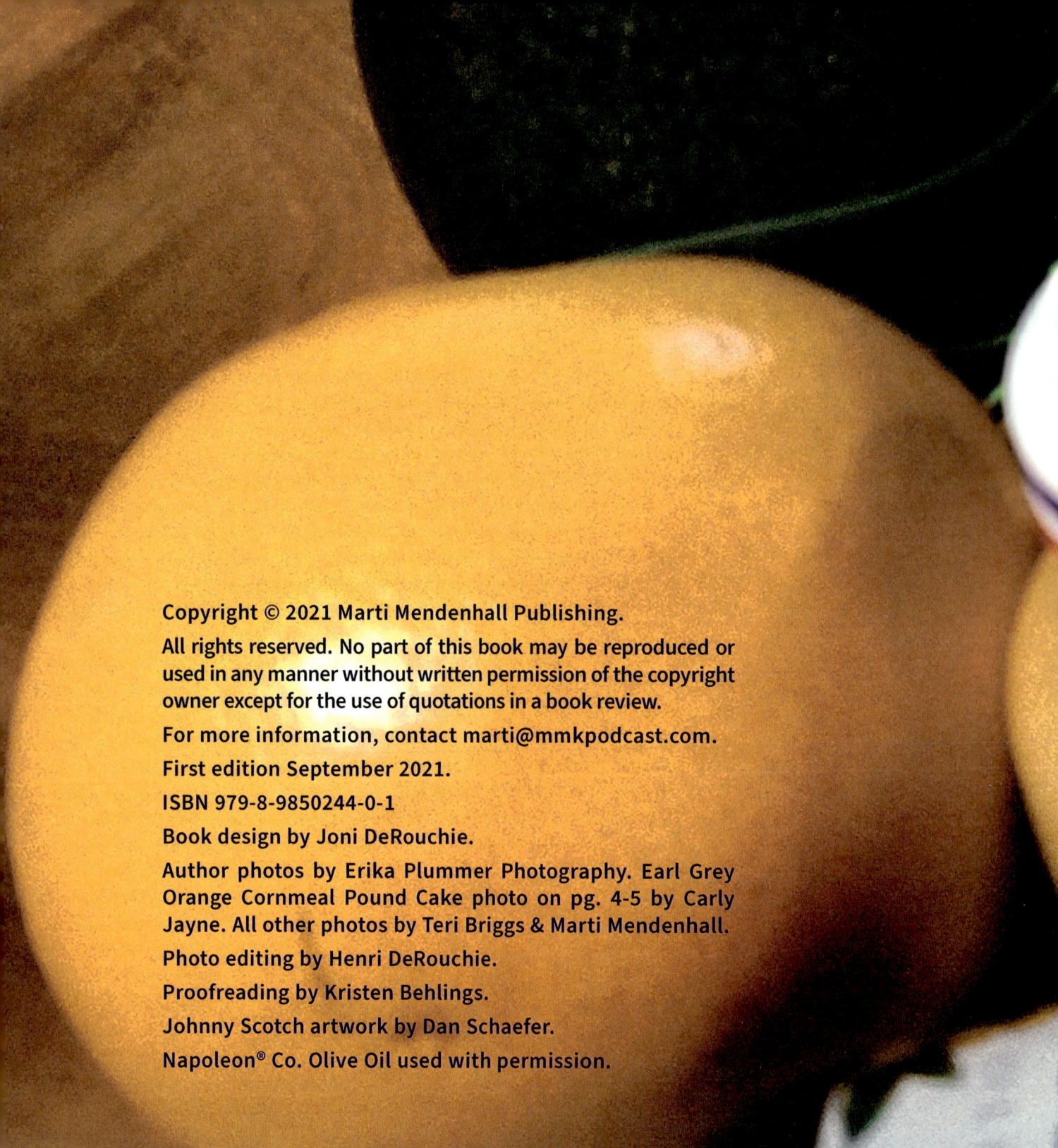

Copyright © 2021 Marti Mendenhall Publishing.

All rights reserved. No part of this book may be reproduced or used in any manner without written permission of the copyright owner except for the use of quotations in a book review.

For more information, contact marti@mmkpodcast.com.

First edition September 2021.

ISBN 979-8-9850244-0-1

Book design by Joni DeRouchie.

Author photos by Erika Plummer Photography. Earl Grey Orange Cornmeal Pound Cake photo on pg. 4-5 by Carly Jayne. All other photos by Teri Briggs & Marti Mendenhall.

Photo editing by Henri DeRouchie.

Proofreading by Kristen Behlings.

Johnny Scotch artwork by Dan Schaefer.

Napoleon® Co. Olive Oil used with permission.

THERE ARE SO MANY FANTASTIC RECIPES IN THIS BOOK; MY TEAM AND I COOK THEM ALL THE TIME. SPEAKING OF MY PRODUCTION TEAM, I WOULDN'T BE HERE WITHOUT THEM! A HUGE THANK YOU TO TERI BRIGGS, PRODUCTION MANAGER; AMER ISSE, RECORDING ENGINEER; AJ MONTOYA, AUDIO EDITOR.

EARL GREY ORANGE CORNMEAL POUND CAKE --- PG 22

WELCOME TO MARTI'S MUSIC KITCHEN!

My name is Marti Mendenhall, and I'm so glad you're here! I'm the creator and host of *Marti's Music Kitchen*—the fun music, food and creativity podcast where anything can happen! This show combines my passion for the creative arts with my appetite for great food, drink and cooking adventures.

It is my philosophy that food and music are the two things that bind us together as people. That's the really great thing about this show. The diversity of guests, of shared experiences, of the many, many different views of food. I delight in the discovery of each interview, the surprises and the tremendous creativity of each dish. The food experience is an adventure in itself.

The podcast episodes are a kick to listen to, sometimes with live performances, a ton of laughter, and lots of amazing food! We've set this book up so you won't miss a thing!

The recipes that follow include QR codes that you can scan to be connected to the corresponding episode of *Marti's Music Kitchen* podcast, links to guests' websites and social media profiles, and links to some of the amazing live performances and fun outtakes on YouTube. You'll also find links to special ingredients used in the recipes and other bonuses at the end of the book.

THANK YOU!

A very special thank you to Naomi LaViolette and John Dover for helping me hatch this plan to turn *Marti's Music Kitchen* into a cookbook. A great idea, indeed! I am also incredibly honored to have Tom D'Antoni, editor of *Oregon Music News*, by my side as a friend, mentor and a hell of a great sounding board when I've needed one. And of course, I thank my family. My partner Todd, my Mom June, my brother Andrew, and a tip of the hat to my Dad Carl, who is gone three years now, but is still etched on my soul as my number-one fan.

If you love the podcast and this cookbook, I am personally inviting YOU to be part of the Marti's Music Kitchen Family! Visit patreon.com/MartiMendenhall TODAY to join the fun and find out about the perks—like special recipes and early access to podcast episodes. You can also find out more about my jazz singing life, my original songs and performances, and sign up for my newsletter featuring a new recipe every month at MartiMendenhall.com.

MARTI MENDENHALL ••• SEPTEMBER 2021

CONTENTS

FOREWORDS BY MARK BITTERMAN & TOM D'ANTONI	08
AMANDA RICHARDS CREAMY POTATO BISQUE, THE ONE COOKIE	10
BEN & HEIDI BETH SADLER FARMER'S MARKET RISOTTO, LEMON BEAN SALAD	12
TOM D'ANTONI RED BEANS & RICE	14
KEN DEROUCHIE SPICY SEAFOOD CORN CHOWDER	16
ZIA MCCABE CAN'T GO WRONG CROCKPOT CHILI	18
ARIETTA WARD CHICKEN VEGETABLE SOUP	20
CARLY JAYNE EARL GREY ORANGE CORNMEAL POUND CAKE	22
SUZANNE NANCE HASH BROWN CRUST QUICHE LORRAINE	24
BO AYARS & DAVID SAFFERT LIBERACE'S STICKY BUNS	26
MARK BITTERMAN RIB EYE STEAKS, MOM'S CAESAR SALAD, WORLD'S BEST MARTINI	28
BRE GREGG & DAN GILDEA FRANGELICO CHALLAH BREAD FRENCH TOAST	30
LARHONDA STEELE GLOOPITY GLOP	32
JOHN DOVER CHILAQUILES, LAZY MAN'S MARGARITA	34
COLIN HOGAN, BRIAN LINK, CHEO LARCOMBE REAL DEAL TUNA MELT, COUSIN MIKEY'S CLAMS	36
JENNI & AMANDA PRICE HEALTHY CHILI TACOS	38
SISTER MERCY MIGAS	40
GREG & CHERIE JOHNSON PASTA CARBONARA	42
TONY STARLIGHT CHICKEN ALFREDO CAULIFLOWER CASSEROLE, KETO GARLIC TOAST	44
SUSANNAH MARS, MERIDETH KAYE CLARK, CHEF JUAN ZARAGOZA CHICKEN PARMESAN	46
MARTI MENDENHALL MARTI-RITA	48
BONUS TREATS	51

FOREWORD BY MARK BITTERMAN

Imagine you're alone, driving through the city. It could be Baltimore. It could be Portland. It could be Palermo. Or Osaka. Or Lagos. It could be the hometown you left long ago, where your friends still drop everything to meet you at a neighborhood café when you return to visit.

You've been driving for awhile. Traffic.

In the rearview mirror you see the honey-colored lava of dusk receding from the black sky's edge. A song is playing on the radio, scratchy and fading out and then back in, gradually gathering itself into a steady ribbon as the signal gathers strength like a train coming around the bend. I don't know what the song is because it's your song, not mine.

I imagine if it were my song it might be "Inner City Blues" by The Christians, though I haven't heard that song on the radio at dusk driving into a city in at least 30 years, or maybe it's "The Sinner", by Isaac Delusion, which I've never heard on the radio. Since it's your song it could be anything…maybe something so obscure that nobody knows it but you and the hopelessly erudite DJ working the graveyard shift at the local college radio station. Whatever.

But the song sticks the moment like an accordion in a Fellini movie, wrapping your past and present, your impulses and your convictions, your regrets and your dreams, into a silken chrysalis where the thinking part of the mind takes the hint and skulks out the back door, leaving the rest of your soul to incubate in stillness for a spell.

There's a sense of "being alive now" that music opens up for us. Laughter, truth, sorrow.

Which is why music and food go so well together. Food is physical. It's dirt and roots and salt and chlorophyll and sometimes chickens—it's the fruits of earthly existence hacked to bits and simmered to perfection in a haze of volatilized garlic. It's a beast. Even when it's vegetables. And it feeds the beast in us, the longing-for, the warmth-seeking, lust-lusting, the hunger that is earthly life.

In music the loopy strands of time assemble into a spotless now. In cooking the vastness of the world recedes and we find ourselves at home, in the homiest of homey places, in our bodies, in the kitchen.

So, music and cooking make intriguing bedfellows. One is about the innermost moment. The other about the centermost place. Stuff the one inside the other like a metaphysical turducken and you get something like **Marti's Music Kitchen**.

There's this woman you don't really know and she's in your house and the radio's playing and you're having a blast and just when you sit down to eat it dawns on you that there's magic to it.

Marti invites herself into the homes of the musically gifted (or in my case, merely music-inspired) where deliciousness and fellowship are in full flower. Join her.

FOREWORD BY TOM D'ANTONI

In 2018 Marti Mendenhall, whom I knew from her singing career, told me she had an idea for a radio show or a podcast combining music and food.

You know the sound a slot machine makes when you hit a jackpot? That's what I heard.

What a great idea!

Six months later, Marti's Music Kitchen premiered to the universe via several avenues including **Oregon Music News**. I was happy to be able to help host the valuable and popular podcast on **OMN**.

The ingredients? One or more musicians or artists in other fields, a recipe or two of their favorite dishes, somewhere to cook them (usually their own kitchens), a dash of good production people and one lively, friendly, talented host to make it a meal (in itself).

Now in its second season (interrupted by quarantine as we all were) Marti had another good idea—this cookbook.

The cool thing is that you can go back and listen to each episode WHILE you're cooking from this cookbook.

Clever, huh? Clever and growing and traveling.

She's based in Oregon, of course, but also has made a road trip to New Orleans with eyes on many other locations in which to find great food and interesting people with whom to cook it.

Marti doesn't walk in with a tightly scripted show; she engages, and—like cooking—combines her own ideas while sticking to the recipe provided by the folks she's talking to.

Hence, the "Anything Can Happen" part of her branding.

In this collection of her first season's episodes she ranges from The Dandy Warhols' Zia McCabe and her "Can't Go Wrong Crockpot Chili," to All Classical Portland CEO Suzanne Nance's "Hash Brown Crust Quiche Lorraine," to Liberace's former band leader Bo Ayars' "Liberace's Sticky Buns," to Soul singer LaRhonda Steele's "Gloopity Glop."

And you'll just have to see (and hear) what that is.

Marti is back in production for season three and everyone is happy about that, anticipating what (literally) stewing over things for the past year plus will bring forth from her.

Meanwhile, happy reading and listening and most of all... eating!

"When I'm not up to my eyeballs producing musicals and writing and stuff, I actually do like to spend a lot of time in the kitchen."

🌐 AMANDARICHARDS.NET
ƒ THEAMANDARICHARDS
▶ AMANDARICHARDSMUSIC
📷 THEGOODLONGWHILES

AMANDA RICHARDS ⋯ THE GOOD LONG WHILES

Amanda is an amazing talent! In addition to cookies, she recently whipped up a musical called *Whistling Dixie*. She's in post-production for the movie version and is writing up a storm of new music! Listen to the episode to hear her live performance, and the truly spooky tales from her time as a chef in a haunted Mt. Hood resort.

THE ONE COOKIE

PREP TIME: 10 MINS ⋯ COOK TIME: 8 MINS ⋯ 12 COOKIES

INGREDIENTS

- 1 cup brown sugar
- ½ cup butter
- 1 tsp salt
- 1 tsp baking soda
- 1 tsp baking powder
- 1 Tbsp bourbon vanilla or extract
- 1½ cups flour
- 1 cup semi-sweet chocolate chips
- ½ cup walnuts (optional)

DIRECTIONS

1. Preheat oven to 375° F.
2. Combine brown sugar, butter, salt, baking soda, baking powder, and vanilla. Blend until mixture reaches a creamy, whipped consistency.
3. Add flour, chocolate chips, and walnuts; mix until blended.
4. Spoon cookies onto an ungreased baking sheet; bake for 8 minutes.

CREAMY POTATO BISQUE

PREP TIME: 10 MINS ⋯ COOK TIME: 30 MINS ⋯ SERVES 5–6

INGREDIENTS

- 2 Tbsp butter
- 1 large onion, chopped
- 2 quarts vegetable stock
- 2 Tbsp sea salt (or to taste)
- 8 medium red potatoes, quartered
- 4 cloves garlic, chopped
- 3 cups arugula, chopped
- Crème fraîche

DIRECTIONS

1. In a large stock pot, sauté chopped onions in butter over low heat until clear or caramelized.
2. Add vegetable stock and salt; bring to a boil.
3. Quarter potatoes and add them to the stock; reduce heat to a simmer.
4. Cook for 20–25 minutes until potatoes are soft.
5. Turn off heat, add chopped garlic and arugula.
6. Using an immersion blender, blend until smooth and creamy.
7. Dish and serve with a dollop of crème fraîche (sour cream or chèvre taste great too).

BEN AND HEIDI BETH SADLER ··· CHASING EBENEZER

SCAN TO LISTEN TO THIS EPISODE

Meeting with Chasing Ebenezer was a delight! I sat down to dinner with band members Heidi Beth and Ben Sadler, Bryan Atkinson, and Ryan Souders. Heidi cooked all afternoon—and voila! Deliciousness! This is one great group of people that truly do consider themselves family. Follow the QR Code, listen to the podcast and hear their LIVE performance on the show.

HEIDI'S FARMERS MARKET RISOTTO

PREP TIME: 10 MINS ··· COOK TIME: 1 HR **SERVES 4**

INGREDIENTS

1 drizzle olive oil

2 Tbsp garlic, diced

1 onion, diced

1½ cups Arborio rice, rinsed

2 cups vegetable or chicken stock

4–6 cups water (varies based on risotto cook time)

⅓ cup white wine

Salt and pepper to taste

Fresh vegetables to sprinkle on top (this uses a handful of freshly chopped basil, cherry tomatoes, and several handfuls of chopped greens–collard, kale, or spinach)

DIRECTIONS

1. Sauté onion and garlic in olive oil in a large pan with a lip of at least 1 inch. Add rice and lightly warm it before adding liquid; set heat to medium or medium-high.

2. Over the next 45 minutes, gradually add stock, water, and wine (if desired). Stir every minute or so until risotto is creamy, but not mushy. Add salt and pepper to taste; you can also add more olive oil or white wine if you desire.

3. Once risotto is creamy, stir in greens and lightly wilt them before removing the risotto from heat.

4. Serve on plates or in shallow bowls, sprinkling the other fresh vegetables on top.

5. Optional: For a richer, non-vegan version, add grated cheese. Serve with my lemon bean salad (next page).

> "For me, music and food means family and community. I lived in Romania for four and a half years, and they just took their time. First you have the soup, and then you have the bread, and it all comes in stages…it's about being together."

HEIDI'S LEMON BEAN SALAD

PREP TIME: 5 MINS ··· MARINATE: 45 MINS **SERVES 4**

SALAD INGREDIENTS

2 cups fully cooked, cooled beans (chickpea, butter, navy, or kidney)

2 cups cooked, cooled corn (I prefer sweet corn)

1 generous handful of chives or green onions, chopped

Salt and pepper to taste

DRESSING INGREDIENTS

1 lemon, juiced (add zest if you want more lemon flavor)

1 Tbsp red wine vinegar

⅛ cup olive oil (or light oil of your choice)

DIRECTIONS

1. Combine salad ingredients in a medium-sized mixing bowl.

2. Combine dressing ingredients in a smaller bowl. Taste the dressing before adding it to the salad; adjust ingredients as needed and add to the salad.

3. Marinate in refrigerator for 45–50 minutes.

4. After marinating, taste and add additional salt if desired.

CHASINGEBENEZER.COM
CHASINGEBENEZER

"Well, you know, Fats Domino used to take all his fixin's and his pots and pans with him on the road and cook up his red beans and rice in his hotel room."

TOM'S TIPS

1. Have guests arrive about an hour before the dish is done.

2. The cheaper the wine, the better (it's not as filtered). Use cheap beer as a substitute.

3. Don't invite your girlfriend over to watch an episode of a freaky food show you produced if you want a girlfriend after she has watched the show.

TOM D'ANTONI ⋯ OREGON MUSIC NEWS & KMHD RADIO

With a career including network TV and radio, newspapers, national magazines, and internet, Tom has wined, dined, and interviewed thousands of musicians—for years as a producer/reporter on OPB's *Oregon Art Beat*, as host of *I Like It Like That* on KMHD Jazz Radio, his podcast *Coffee Shop Conversations*, and as editor of *Oregon Music News*. His stories are epic and he is one of the most interesting people I've ever known!

SCAN TO LISTEN TO THIS EPISODE

BUSTER HOLMES' RED BEANS & RICE (WITH TOM'S TWEAKS) — PREP TIME: OVERNIGHT ⋯ COOK TIME: 5 HRS — SERVES 4-6

INGREDIENTS

- 2 lb red beans
- 3 cups Sauterne (or sweet wine of choice)
- 1-2 medium onions, chopped
- ½ green pepper, chopped
- 1 lb smoked ham hock
- 1-2 cloves garlic, chopped
- Hot sauce to taste
- Salt and pepper to taste
- 1 pot cooked rice

DIRECTIONS

1. Soak washed, rock-free beans in Sauterne or alternative wine overnight (the cheaper, the better–it's not as filtered).
2. In a large pot, cover beans with water (you can also use some of the sauce you soaked them in).
3. Add onions, green pepper, ham hock, and garlic.
4. Cook for 5 hours over low heat, stirring once per hour and adding hot sauce to taste.
5. Serve over rice–any kind of rice will do!

HEAR TOM'S INTERVIEW WITH MARTI ON "COFFEE SHOP CONVERSATIONS"
MMKCOOKBOOK.COM/MARTI-COFFEESHOP

🌐 OREGONMUSICNEWS.COM
🌐 KMHD.ORG

15

KEN DEROUCHIE ··· THE KEN DEROUCHIE BAND

SCAN TO LISTEN TO THIS EPISODE

I have never laughed so hard during an interview! Check out the outtakes for this episode and you'll laugh, too. Ken is an absolutely outstanding cook, with a taste for the finest brandy and a great cigar. I felt really fortunate that this episode was also featured on our local KOIN 6 evening news. Not to mention that this is hands-down the best seafood chowder I have ever tasted! Five stars in my book.

KEN'S SPICY SEAFOOD CORN CHOWDER

PREP TIME: 30 MINS ··· COOK TIME: 1 HR ··· SERVES 10-12

INGREDIENTS

- 1 qt half-and-half
- 1 qt heavy cream
- 1–2 Tbsp Better Than Bouillon® Lobster Base (see pg. 50 for link)
- 2 cans whole kernel corn (or 6 ears of corn, roasted on the grill)
- 1 can creamed corn
- ⅓ cup sugar
- 1 tsp Chile de árbol powder
- 2 poblano or pasilla peppers
- 1 medium yellow onion, peeled and quartered
- 5 stalks celery, chopped into 4 pieces
- 2 sticks butter
- 1 cup flour
- 2 raw lobster tails
- 1 lb raw shrimp—thawed, peeled, and deveined (refrigerate until needed)

MAKING THE BASE

1. Add half-and-half and heavy cream to a large pot on medium heat. Add Lobster Base and whisk in.
2. Drain cans of whole kernel corn (or cut corn off ears), add to pot.
3. Add creamed corn to pot. Stir regularly with a wire whisk.
4. Add sugar and continue to stir.
5. Add Chile de árbol powder and mix well. Add more Chile de árbol powder to your desired heat level (I like to use a lot more). Continue to stir regularly. Once the pot begins to simmer, reduce heat to low.
6. Roast peppers on the grill, lightly charring all sides until you can easily peel them. Once peeled, core and de-seed peppers and chop into small pieces before adding to the pot.
7. Put onion and celery in a blender. Add water and puree for about 20 seconds. Use a tight weave strainer and strain the liquid out of the puree. Take the pulp/puree that is left and add it to the pot.
8. Continue to stir regularly.

> "I decided 5 years ago that I wanted to try to do something for the community. The thing that I kind of latched onto was the Oregon Food Bank. I think we got about eighteen hundred pounds of food donated last year, and then we had close to $2500 in donations. So that, for just the one year, the total came out to something like 12,000 meals."

- 🌐 KDBAND.NET
- ⓕ KENDEROUCHIEBAND
- ☁ KEN-DEROUCHIE-BAND

WATCH: LINKS.MMKCOOKBOOK.COM/KEN-OUTTAKES

MAKING A ROUX

1. Melt butter in a pan over medium heat (do not let it burn).
2. Once the butter is melted, add flour. Mix until it is smooth and creamy. Constantly mix this so the butter doesn't burn.
3. Add this mixture to the pot and stir for about 2 minutes. This will thicken the liquid into thick, hearty chowder. Continue to stir regularly.

FINALIZING

1. Lay the lobster tails on a cutting board with the bottom of the tail facing up. Use a sharp knife to cut a line, top to bottom through the bottom layer of scales. Peel back the shell and scoop out the meat. Cut the tail meat into small pieces. Do not add this until about 5 minutes before you're ready to eat.

ADD THE SEAFOOD

1. Once everything is mixed and you have the right flavor and thickness, you can add the shrimp and lobster 3–5 minutes before you are ready to serve. Don't put the seafood in too soon or it will become overcooked and rubbery.
2. Serve with warm crusty bread.

- DANDYWARHOLS.COM
- ATOZIAREALESTATE.COM
- THEDJRESCUE
- ZIAMCCABE

"If you were relying on this to pay your bills, it's so easy to zap some of that joy. And that's how I started to feel about music, is like...man, I want to play music, not work music."

ZIA MCCABE ··· THE DANDY WARHOLS

Zia is well-known for her musical talents on synth, bass, and percussion for The Dandy Warhols. She is also a successful real estate agent for Windermere, as "A to Zia" Real Estate in Portland, Oregon. In addition, she's also been "saving good parties from bad music since 2001" as DJ RESCUE. She has a warm, open personailty that made this interview really click!

SCAN TO LISTEN TO THIS EPISODE

ZIA'S CAN'T GO WRONG CROCKPOT CHILI

PREP TIME: 20 MINS ··· COOK TIME: 6-8 HRS   SERVES 8-10

INGREDIENTS

WATCH: LINKS.MMKCOOKBOOK.COM/ZIA-OUTTAKES

2–2½ lbs ground beef

2 large sweet potatoes, diced

4–6 large carrots, chopped

1–3 peppers of your choice (jalapeño, cherry bomb, etc), chopped

1–2 bell peppers (any color), chopped

1 head garlic, minced

1 Red onion, chopped

1 28 oz can fire roasted tomatoes

2–3 8oz cans tomato sauce

2–3 cups bone or beef broth

2 Tbsp chili powder

Herbs and spices to taste (thyme, oregano, red chili pepper flakes, cayenne pepper, cumin, salt and pepper)

DIRECTIONS

1. Over medium heat, cook beef in skillet, seasoning with salt and pepper.
2. Add beef and other ingredients to Crockpot and cook on low heat for 6–8 hours. Freezes well.

ARIETTA WARD ⋯ JAZZ SONGSTRESS

This jazz songstress and cosmetologist is also the daughter of celebrated musician Janice Scroggins. Well-known for her cooking Instagram posts and her passion for good food, Mz. Etta is the star of her kitchen with this great homestyle recipe.

ARIETTA'S CHICKEN VEGETABLE SOUP

PREP TIME: 20 MINS ⋯ COOK TIME: 50 MINS — SERVES 5-6

INGREDIENTS

- 2 Tbsp soy sauce or tamari
- Sambal to taste
- 1 tsp apple cider vinegar
- 1-2 Tbsp butter
- 1-2 Tbsp vegetable oil
- 1 package chicken thighs, bone in
- Salt and pepper to taste
- 2-3 cloves garlic, minced
- 3 stalks celery with leaves, chopped
- 3-4 carrots, chopped; peeled if desired
- 1 medium onion, chopped
- 1 head bok choy, stems and leaves chopped
- 1-2 heads broccoli, chopped
- 1 green bell pepper, chopped
- 1 red bell pepper, chopped
- 1 large zucchini, chopped
- 1 Scotch bonnet pepper, chopped (optional) or habanero or jalapeño
- Ocho Rios® Scotch Bonnet Hot Pepper Sauce to taste
- 2 cubes chicken bouillon

DIRECTIONS

1. Prepare sauce mixture: Combine soy sauce, sambal, and apple cider vinegar in a small bowl.

2. In a large nonstick pot, warm butter and vegetable oil over medium heat.

3. Season chicken thighs with salt and pepper. Sear on both sides for approx. 5-10 minutes. While chicken thighs are browning add garlic, some of the celery and carrot, and half of the onion. Once seared, remove chicken thighs from pot and set aside.

4. Layer vegetables in pot in the following order: bok choy, remaining carrots, broccoli, remaining celery, other half of the onion, bell pepper, zucchini. (For spicier soup, add scotch bonnet pepper, habanero, or jalapeño; layer between onions and bell pepper).

5. Add chicken thighs, bouillon cubes, sauce mixture, and enough water to cover everything.

6. Simmer for 10 minutes and then remove bones from chicken thighs.

7. Return chicken thighs to pot and add water; simmer for another 15 minutes or until chicken is completely cooked.

> "That's the way I was raised. You know, waking up, I would hear my Mom do her Hannon Scales, or I would hear the Gap Band or Zapp & Roger, or Middle-Eastern belly dance music…it doesn't matter. Music is music. To be open to that—to know that there is no limitation in music—so why should there be a limitation on you?"

MZETTASWORLD.COM

GET THE HOT SAUCE ··· PG. 50

> "So the reason why the scale is really important for baking is because...if you sat down and just measured six cups of flour and weighed each cup, each one is going to be different. When it comes to cakes and things where you really need to have accuracy, and you need it to turn out perfectly and consistently, you are only really going to get that with a volume measure."

INGREDIENTS

2 bags Earl Grey tea (or other preferred tea)

1 cups hot water

1 cup sugar

3 medium oranges (or other citrus fruits such as mandarin oranges, blood oranges, or lemons. If using smaller citrus, add 1–2 additional fruits.)

8 oz salted butter, room temperature (2 sticks)

8 oz sugar (about 1 cup and 1 Tbsp)

8 oz eggs, room temperature (about 4 large eggs and one white)

1 pinch salt

8 oz cornmeal (about 1⅓ cup)

LOVELIKESALT.COM
LOVELIKESALT

CARLY JAYNE ⋯ LOVE LIKE SALT

Carly Jayne is a food stylist and photographer, recipe developer, and owner of Love Like Salt. It's a cooking education, as Carly teaches us how to develop a recipe using formulas. She specializes in creative storytelling through food photography and design. That's right—she styles food for a living! Talented and fun, Carly created a recipe to die for.

SCAN TO LISTEN TO THIS EPISODE

EARL GREY ORANGE CORNMEAL POUND CAKE
PREP TIME: 15 MINS ⋯ COOK TIME: 1 HR · SERVES 12

DIRECTIONS

Note: A kitchen scale is highly recommended. Once you start baking with a scale, you'll never want to go back to cups and spoons!

1. Heat oven to 350° F.
2. Prepare 8" round cake pan with a circle of parchment or silicone sheet in the bottom. Butter well.
3. Brew tea in hot water for 3-5 minutes and then add to a large, shallow frying pan.
4. Stir in 1 cup sugar and simmer on medium heat until dissolved, stirring occasionally.
5. Meanwhile, slice two oranges as thinly as possible (hold the remaining fruit for zest). Add slices to simmering syrup and keep an eye on them as you make batter; they are done when soft and translucent. They should taste pleasantly sweet and slightly bitter from the candied peel.
6. Remove from heat and place slices on the bottom of the prepared cake pan in a circular pattern, covering the entire bottom. Keep any leftover oranges to decorate the finished cake (reserve syrup for cocktails or sodas).
7. Cream butter on medium speed in stand mixer for approx. 1-7 minutes. Add 8 oz sugar, continue to cream until fluffy. Add orange zest to mixture with a pinch of salt. Set mixer to slow and add eggs one at a time (add the next egg once the previous one has been worked in smoothly). Gently fold in cornmeal until just incorporated.
8. Pour batter into the pan over the oranges and smooth the top with a spatula.
9. Bake at 350°. Start to check cake at 35 minutes. The sides should pull away and a toothpick should come out clean.
10. Remove from the oven, let cool for a few minutes. Slide a knife between the cake and the pan. Place a cooling rack on top of the pan and flip the cake over. Remove the parchment or silicon sheet from the top of cake and use remaining orange slices to fill any gaps or cover imperfections if desired.

SCAN TO LISTEN TO THIS EPISODE

SUZANNE NANCE ⋯ PRESIDENT, ALL CLASSICAL PORTLAND

What an honor to interview Suzanne Nance, Portland's Queen of Classical. She is an award-winning broadcaster, amazingly talented soprano, President and CEO of All-Classical Portland and host of Sunday Brunch. Suzanne sang LIVE on the podcast, with David Saffert as her accompanist. I even joined her for a scat or two! The hashbrown crust is a must-try, by the way.

HASH BROWN CRUST QUICHE LORRAINE

PREP TIME: 30 MINS ⋯ COOK TIME: 1 HR SERVES 8

HASH BROWN CRUST INGREDIENTS

- 1 package frozen organic hash brown potatoes, thawed
- 1 lb butter
- 1 egg
- ½ cup cheddar cheese, shredded
- ½ cup Parmesan cheese, grated
- 1 tsp coarse salt
- ¼ tsp pepper

DIRECTIONS

1. Preheat the oven to 400° F.

2. Squeeze excess moisture from hash browns. Mix in a bowl with butter, egg, cheese, salt and pepper.

3. In a 9-inch greased baking pan, pat mixture into bottom and up sides of pan.

4. Reduce to 375° F and bake approx. 20–25 minutes or until sides turn to golden brown and crisp.

> "I was thinking, you know, why not make quiche, and why not make it friendly for our gluten-free friends. I'm not a gluten-free person, but I have so many friends who are. So the idea of a hash brown crust…it's healthier, and it's really tasty and it's gluten-free!"

WATCH THE LIVE PERFORMANCE:
LINKS.MMKCOOKBOOK.COM/SUZANNE

🌐 SUZANNENANCE.COM
🌐 ALLCLASSICAL.ORG
ƒ SAFFERTSANSSEQUINS (DAVID)

QUICHE LORRAINE INGREDIENTS

- 4 strips bacon
- 1 onion, thinly sliced
- 1 cup Gruyère or Swiss cheese, cubed
- ¼ cup parmesan cheese, grated
- 4 eggs, lightly beaten
- 2 cups heavy cream (or 1 cup milk and 1 cup cream)
- ¼ tsp nutmeg
- ½ tsp salt
- ¼ tsp pepper, freshly ground
- Tabasco® sauce to taste

DIRECTIONS

1. Cook bacon until crisp and remove from skillet. Remove all but one tablespoon of bacon fat from skillet.
2. Cook onion in fat until transparent.
3. Crumble bacon. Sprinkle bacon, onion, and cheeses over the inside of the hash brown crust.
4. Combine eggs, cream, nutmeg, salt, pepper and Tabasco sauce to taste, then strain the mixture over the onion-cheese mixture.
5. Slide the pie onto a baking sheet. Bake the pie until a knife inserted one inch from the pastry edge comes out clean (approx. 25 minutes).
6. Remove to a wire rack and let stand 5–10 minutes before serving.

WATCH THE LIVE PERFORMANCE:
LINKS.MMKCOOKBOOK.COM/MMK-DAVID

"Before I get on stage," says David, "and I'm in sequins from head to toe, and the hair, a wig and the makeup and the rings, and I hear Bo and the band will start playing the Liberace Hilton-Vegas intro, it just puts you in the mindset to be him."

BO AYARS & DAVID SAFFERT ⋯ LIBERACE & LIZA TRIBUTE

Liberace was famous for his over-the-top performance style, but did you know he also liked to cook? Pianist David Saffert brings the costumes, music, and glamour of Liberace to his marvelous tribute to Mr. Showmanship. Joining him is Bo Ayars, who was Liberace's music director for 13 years. Together they bring new life to one of Li's favorite recipes—sticky buns! Be sure to listen to the podcast...oh the stories they tell!

SCAN TO LISTEN TO THIS EPISODE

LIBERACE'S STICKY BUNS (AS BEST BO CAN REMEMBER AND DAVID CAN INFER)

PREP TIME: 15 MINS ⋯ COOK TIME: 20–30 MINS ⋯ MAKES 24 BUNS

INGREDIENTS

- 1¼ cup white raisins
- ¼ cup light rum
- 2 sticks unsalted butter (or salted for zing)
- 1½ tsp pumpkin pie spice (or to taste), or:
    - ½ tsp cinnamon
    - ¼ tsp nutmeg
    - ¼ tsp allspice
    - ¼ tsp cloves
    - ¼ tsp ginger (for a little bite)
- 1½ cups brown sugar
- 1 cup pecans, roughly chopped
- 3 packages refrigerated unbaked rolls (crescent, cinnamon, or similar)

DIRECTIONS

1. Preheat oven to 325° F.
2. Soak raisins in rum until soft. Microwave 15–35 seconds to soften if needed.
3. In a small pot, melt butter, spices, and brown sugar over low heat. Stir until thick and bubbly.
4. Line two greased non-stick cupcake pans with the bigger chunks of pecans.
5. Add 1 tablespoon of the butter mix to each cup.
6. Flatten rolls into a sheet of dough using a rolling pin; brush butter mixture on to the dough (about ¼ of the pot). Scatter raisins and chopped pecans on top of the dough.
7. Roll dough into a log, slice off 1–1¼" sections and place into baking pan cups.
8. Bake 13–15 minutes or until the buns begin to brown on top.
9. Remove from oven. Place a plate over the baking pan and flip it over to release the buns onto the plate. Eat them warm!

Note: Use first batch to determine how much butter mixture to put in the cups for the second batch.

- ax2music.com (BO)
- liberaceandliza.com
- LIBERACEANDLIZA
- LIBERACEANDLIZA

SCAN TO LISTEN TO THIS EPISODE

MARK BITTERMAN ··· BITTERMAN SALT CO. & THE MEADOW

Mark is a James Beard Award-winning food writer, selmelier, and chef with store locations in Portlland, NYC, and Tokyo. He is the most genuine of people, and a true explorer of salt and good food! If you try his martini recipe, be prepared—it was so strong, I didn't know if I could make it through the interview! Not to mention, the Caesar salad recipe was handed down from his mother. Precious cargo in this cookbook.

RIB EYE STEAKS

PREP TIME: 2 HRS ··· COOK TIME: 15-20 MINS — SERVES 2

1. Start with 2 nice-sized steaks. Ours were about 1.5" thick.
2. Pick a great salt or two, something with a story to tell!
3. Sprinkle salt and rub into both sides of meat.
4. Let sit at room temperature for 1–2 hours.
5. In cast iron skillet on high, cook steaks in 2 tablespoons butter, approximately 5 min per side. (It will be smoky!)
6. Finish with a blowtorch to give it a beautiful brown crust.
7. Let steaks rest for 1–2 minutes. Scatter coarse salt over steaks and serve.

> "I meet this salt maker and he's this guy who's got this sandy blonde hair and he has blue sun-bleached eyes...he's looking out over the horizon and telling me how he makes salt with his hands and the sea and the sun. And I'm like...who are you?"

THE WORLD'S BEST MARTINI

PREP TIME: 5 MINS

1. In a large beaker with a LOT of ice, mix 1 part vermouth and 5 parts gin.
2. Always stir the batch! (not shaken) Stir frozen ice longer than bar ice.
3. Pour into glass; garnish with olives.
4. Raise your glass and make a toast!

🌐 MARKBITTERMAN.COM
🌐 BITTERMANSALT.CO

MARK'S BOOKS:
THEMEADOW.COM/COLLECTIONS/BOOKS

CAESAR SALAD

PREP TIME: 15 MINS … COOK TIME: 20 MINS   SERVES 4

INGREDIENTS

Romaine lettuce

2 egg yolks

2–3 whole lemons, juiced

2–3 cloves garlic, pressed

1 dollop of Dijon mustard

A TON of black pepper

Several anchovies, minced; and oil from the anchovies

Olive oil

Vegetable oil

Croutons

1 cup Parmigiano and Reggiano cheese, grated

DIRECTIONS

1. Chop romaine lettuce to preferred size, add to bowl.

2. In a quart jar, add egg yolks and lemon juice. Cover jar and shake until yolks are broken. Let mixture sit for 3 minutes.

3. Add garlic and Dijon mustard. Cover jar and shake.

4. Add black pepper, anchovy oil, and desired amount of anchovies. Add olive oil and vegetable oil. Add croutons.

5. Cover jar and shake until thoroughly mixed.

6. Pour dressing over salad and toss until lettuce is coated. Sprinkle grated cheese over the salad and toss again.

Note: You can make your own croutons by cutting old French or sourdough bread into cubes, drizzling with olive oil, and toasting until golden brown.

"This is a song that's all about how we work super hard to get to someplace in life, and then when we get there we realize that it didn't matter at all," say Bre of a song they composed together for their upcoming CD. "The only thing that matters is the loved ones in your life and living right now in the present moment."

🌐 REDBIRDSOUL.COM
ⓕ REDBIRDSOUL
▶ BREGREGG
📷 REDBIRDSOUL

WATCH: LINKS.MMKCOOKBOOK.COM/REDBIRD-OUTTAKES

BRE GREGG AND DAN GILDEA ··· RED BIRD SOUL

These two are musical geniuses—and the Frangelico French Toast is not far behind! I would describe this duo as one funky, beautiful and bluesy package! It blows me away at how these two make being successful musicians and successful parents look so...graceful. How do they do it all and manage to cook breakfast? Give it a listen to the podcast and find out!

FRANGELICO CHALLAH BREAD FRENCH TOAST

PREP TIME: 10 MINS ··· COOK TIME: 15 MINS   SERVES 4-5

INGREDIENTS

8 eggs

¾ cup milk or fresh cream

1 Tbsp sugar or maple syrup

1 cup Frangelico® liqueur (see pg. 50 for link)

Kosher salt (optional, up to 1½ tsp)

Unsalted sweet cream butter

1 loaf challah, sliced thick

Whipped cream

Maple syrup

DIRECTIONS

1. In a large mixing bowl, add eggs, milk, sugar (or maple syrup), Frangelico®, and salt (if using). Mix with a whisk or fork until blended.

2. Heat a large cast iron skillet over medium-high heat and add a generous amount of butter to the pan.

3. Dip slices of challah in egg mixture, set slices in pan and brown on both sides.

4. Serve with maple syrup and whipped cream. Even better with fresh fruit and sausage!

LaRhonda Steele ⋯ First Lady of Portland Blues

SCAN TO LISTEN TO THIS EPISODE

LaRhonda will forever be part of my heart, as she was my first guest on the *Marti's Music Kitchen* podcast. She was recently inducted into the Oregon Music Hall of Fame for her outstanding contributions to gospel, soul and R&B music. LaRhonda has shared her amazing vocals and graceful charm locally and internationally for decades. Listen to the podcast with special guest and daughter Lo Steele. Hear how the heart-healthy recipe for Gloopity Glop became a family household favorite!

LaRhonda's Gloopity Glop

PREP TIME: 20 MINS ⋯ COOK TIME: 25 MINS ⋯ SERVES 4

INGREDIENTS

½ cup olive oil

1 sweet potato, diced

1 russet potato, diced

1 package andouille chicken sausage, diced

1 red onion, diced

1 red pepper, cut into strips

1 green pepper, cut into strips

3 cups kale

Salt and pepper to taste

DIRECTIONS

1. Over medium heat, fry both sweet and russet potatoes in 1 Tbsp of olive oil in a large skillet until brown. Remove from skillet.
2. Brown sausage.
3. Add onions, peppers, and remaining olive oil.
4. Add kale and browned potatoes, heat until kale is softened.
5. Add salt and pepper to taste.
6. Yummy time!

> "I'm not as much afraid of creativity as I was, because when you go for your sixth surgery, and you say, 'Am I going to wake up?' And you wake up and you're not so afraid of the little things anymore."

- 🌐 LARHONDASTEELE.COM
- ⓕ LARHONDA.STEELE
- ▷ LINKS.MMKCOOKBOOK.COM/LOSTEELE-SPOTIFY
- ⓘ LOSTEELE

- 🌐 JOHNDMUSIC.COM
- 🌐 READJOHNDOVER.COM
- ⓕ JOHNDOVERTRUMPET
- 🐦 JOHNNYSCOTCHJUSTICE

LAZY MAN'S PIÑA COLADA

Combine in a blender until foamy:

4 cups of ice
16 oz coconut rum
1–1½ cups frozen pineapple chunks

Makes 1–3 servings

"Cooking with the heart is how we learn to show people what we think of them...It also forces you as the chef to engage and indulge in what you're creating to make it better."

JOHN DOVER ··· MUSICIAN & AUTHOR

I've played with my good friend John—jazz trumpeter and endorsed Bach Artist—many times over the years. This Renaissance man grew up cooking, so his recipes are tried and true. I can't wait for you to try the piña colada! John also has a successful career as the comic book author of the booze-drinking, lady-loving detective known as "Johnny Scotch." He's even been featured at Comic-Con!

CHILAQUILES

PREP TIME: 10 MINS ··· COOK TIME: 15 MINS · SERVES 2-3

INGREDIENTS

Vegetable or avocado oil

1 cup green chile salsa

Tortilla chips (see directions to make your own)

Eggs, 2 per serving

1 bunch cilantro, chopped

Chèvre or queso fresco, crumbled

Kosher salt

DIRECTIONS

1. Heat a large skillet over medium-high heat. Coat skillet with approx. 2 Tbsp oil.
2. Add salsa and tortilla chips. Mix until chips are coated, but still crispy. Pour out onto plate.
3. In another skillet, cook eggs sunny side up.
4. Put eggs on top of chips and garnish with cilantro and crumbled cheese.
5. Variations: Add shredded rotisserie chicken, black or refried beans, and/or pickled jalapeños. You can also use red salsa instead of green, or a mix of both.

HOMEMADE TORTILLA CHIPS

1. Preheat oven to broil (high broil for ovens with high/low broil settings).
2. Lightly oil 12 corn tortillas and sprinkle with kosher salt.
3. Broil tortillas until crisp and brown.
4. Let cool, then break tortillas into smaller pieces.

SCAN TO LISTEN TO THIS EPISODE

COLIN HOGAN, BRIAN LINK, CHEO LARCOMBE ⋯ THE COLIN TRIO

Have you ever cooked in a cast iron skillet that is over 100 years old? Neither had I! This tight-knit group takes their sultry Southern influences into the Kitchen to make the luscious layers of the "The Real Deal Tuna Melt," made in a cast iron skillet handed down through three generations of Brian's family. And it has to be said that Mikey's clams are some of the BEST I've ever had!

THE REAL DEAL TUNA MELT

🕐 COOK TIME: 30 MINS   🍴 SERVES 3

INGREDIENTS

- 1 lb tuna steaks
- 1 Tbsp olive oil
- Salt and pepper to taste
- 1 Tbsp dill relish
- 1-2 Tbsp mayonnaise
- 1 Tbsp mustard (yellow and/or deli)
- 1 tsp chili powder
- Kaiser rolls
- Provolone cheese slices, 1 per sandwich
- Tomato slices, 1-2 per sandwich

DIRECTIONS

1. Preheat oven to 375°.
2. Rub tuna steaks with oil and sprinkle with fresh ground pepper.
3. In a cast iron skillet, heat oil over high heat until almost smoking. Sear tuna steaks in pan, flipping once halfway through.
4. Once tuna is seared, remove skillet from stove and place in oven, cooking tuna until it is no longer pink. Remove from oven and let cool.
5. Set oven to broil.
6. Once cooled, crumble tuna with fork in a mixing bowl. Add dill relish, mayonnaise, mustard, and chili powder; mix thoroughly.
7. Slice Kaiser rolls and spread mayo on only one half of each; toast the other halves under broiler. Place tuna on mayo side of roll. Cover tuna mixture with folded cheese slices and place under broiler until cheese begins to brown.
8. Spread mayonnaise on toasted halves.
9. Place a slice of tomato between tuna and cheese.

Optional: Add chipotle seasoning to tuna mixture for a spicier sandwich.

"When Brian says he's cooked something, you want to try it. No need to ask what it is." –Cheo

THECOLINTRIO.COM
THECOLINTRIO
FEISTYFOLK
THE_COLIN_TRIO

COUSIN MIKEY'S CLAMS — SERVES 3

INGREDIENTS

- 1 can Budweiser® beer
- ½ lemon, sliced
- 2 cloves garlic, finely chopped
- 1 stick butter
- 1 Tbsp Old Bay® Seasoning (see pg. 50 for link)
- 2 lbs fresh little neck clams
- 1 baguette, sliced

DIRECTIONS

1. In a medium saucepan, heat beer over medium heat.
2. Add lemon slices, garlic, butter, and Old Bay® Seasoning. Bring mixture to a boil. Add clams and cook approx. 4 minutes.
3. Pour entire mixture into a bowl to cool.
4. Eat the clams and dip the sliced baguette in the sauce.

"I think the coolest part about cooking is when you cook with love, you taste the love!" says Amanda. "Regardless of how many people come into the kitchen with you, if you can make something with love, then they can feel like they are at home with whatever it is you cooked."

🌐 THEAMMUSIC.COM
ƒ ACOUSTICMINDSMUSIC
☁ ACOUSTICMINDSMUSIC
📷 _THEAM & MCJOJOLOVESYOU

JENNI & AMANDA PRICE ⋯ THE ACOUSTIC MINDS

SCAN TO LISTEN TO THIS EPISODE

We were literally dancing in the kitchen with these identical twin sisters, Jenny and Amanda Price. These two have been rocking the Electronic Dance Music world and have a notable following all along the West Coast. The tacos? Their travel FAVE when they are commuting from Portland to L.A.!

JENNI & AMANDA'S HEALTHY CHILI TACOS

PREP TIME: 20 MINS ⋯ COOK TIME: 45 MINS   SERVES 6-8

INGREDIENTS

2 yellow onions, chopped

2 yellow or orange bell peppers, chopped

3 lbs ground turkey

3 packages Lawry's® taco seasoning

2 red peppers, chopped

1 4 oz can Ortega® diced hot jalapeños

2 15 oz cans golden corn

1 15 oz can black beans

1 15 oz can kidney beans

3 15 oz cans diced tomatoes (with or without green chiles or jalapeños)

1 15 oz can fire roasted tomatoes

3 4 oz cans diced chiles

2 jalapeño peppers, sliced

DIRECTIONS

1. In a large skillet, cook bell peppers and one onion over medium heat. Set aside.
2. In another skillet, add turkey and the other onion; season with salt and pepper. Once cooked, add taco seasoning and stir.
3. Add remaining onions, red peppers, and diced hot jalapeños to turkey and simmer.
4. Once the mixture has cooked down, combine with onion/pepper mixture from step 1.
5. In a separate pot, add corn, beans, tomatoes, chilies, and sliced jalapeños; cook approx. 10 mins.

SISTER MERCY ⋯ RHYTHM & BLUES BAND

Sister Mercy blows me away every time I hear them. I felt especially lucky to have Roger prep his mother's heirloom recipe for Migas. They are so good, my crew and I now make them all the time! This interview was particularly special, as they did a LIVE performance on the show. They treat each other as family and food is part of the deal.

MIGAS

PREP TIME: 10 MINS ⋯ COOK TIME: 15 MINS   SERVES 3–4

INGREDIENTS

Salsa (see next page)

¼ cup vegetable oil

4–6 corn tortillas per serving

2 eggs

½ cup Mexican cheese (cotija, oaxaca, queso fresco, etc)

DIRECTIONS

1. Prepare the salsa (as shown on opposite page)
2. Heat oil In a large skillet over medium-high heat.
3. Tear tortillas into bite-sized pieces and fry until crispy.
4. In a small bowl, beat two eggs.
5. Reduce heat to medium. Pour eggs into pan; stir until cooked.
6. Add 2–3 Tbsp salsa and top with cheese.

🌐 **SISTERMERCY.ROCKS**
ƒ **SISTERMERCYPDX**

WATCH THE LIVE PERFORMANCE:
LINKS.MMKCOOKBOOK.COM/SISTER-MERCY

SALSA

Combine ingredients in a blender until chunky:

1 24 oz can petite diced tomatoes

2 jalapeño peppers, whole with tops cut off

1 bunch cilantro, cleaned and de-stemmed

3 Tbsp olive oil

3–4 cloves garlic

Salt to taste

"Debby and Roger are like the band 'Mom and Dad'," says lead singer April Brown. "I call Debby 'Band-Mom' (or older sister), in terms of, like…it's their home and they take care of us. They house us if we have to stay the night. I think food brings everybody together. So we feel like a family. Definitely."

- 🌐 CASCADEBLUESASSOCIATION.ORG
- Ⓕ GREG.S.JOHNSON.9
- Ⓕ CASCADEBLUESASSOCIATION

PASTA CARBONARA INGREDIENTS

1 lb pasta (see opposite page)

1 egg

½ cup half-and-half

Sea salt and fresh ground black pepper to taste

12 slices pancetta (or 12 slices smoked streaky bacon)

1 cup fresh or frozen peas

2 sprigs fresh mint, leaves picked and finely sliced

Parmesan cheese, grated

PASTA CARBONARA DIRECTIONS

1. Bring a large pot of water to a boil.

2. Add pasta and cook al dente (approx. 10 minutes).

3. In a mixing bowl, add egg, half-and-half, salt, and pepper; whisk until combined and set aside.

4. In a large skillet, fry pancetta until crispy and golden.

5. When pasta has approx. 1½ minutes of cook time remaining, add peas to pot.

6. Strain pasta and peas in a colander; set aside some of the water.

7. Add pasta to pancetta and stir in most of the mint. If the pan isn't big enough, combine pasta, pancetta, and mint in a large warmed bowl.

8. Add egg/cream mixture to pasta (add while pasta is still hot so that it cooks the egg/cream mixture to a silky smooth consistency). Toss together and loosen with a small amount of pasta water if needed.

9. Salt and pepper to taste, top with Parmesan cheese and mint.

CHERIE AND GREG "SLIM LIVELY" JOHNSON

This was my first time making pasta from scratch. Cherie was there to coach me every step of the way. It was totally worth the effort! This interview stands out as we got a sneak peek at Greg's photography collections and some of his musical achievements. The accolades are outstanding—and so is Cherie's authentic Italian dish!

PASTA CARBONARA

PREP TIME: 1 HR ⋯ COOK TIME: 20 MINS **SERVES 4**

PASTA INGREDIENTS

2½ **cups all-purpose flour**

2½ **cups semolina flour**

7 eggs

PASTA DIRECTIONS

1. Sift flour into a large mixing bowl. Make a well in the middle, add eggs and mix gently until incorporated.
2. Place on floured surface and knead 7–8 minutes.
3. Let dough rest 30 minutes, then divide into portions to be put through pasta maker (or hand-roll into desired noodle shape).

Dough can be kneaded in a stand mixer instead of by hand.

> "All of her meals are my favorite! I love everything she cooks."

TONY STARLIGHT ⋯ PERFORMER, AMATEUR ORNITHOLOGIST

Brett Kucera created Tony Starlight—his crooning lounge singer alter ego—in Portland dives in the '90s. He opened the Tony Starlight Supperclub (now Showroom) in 2007, where he developed his act into a world-class music and comedy performance. He is also a bird photographer and features his best shots in an annual calendar. Tony credits the ketogenic diet for bringing out his younger, more handsome self! I wasn't a "keto" fan until *after* I tried these dishes. OMG, so good!

CHICKEN ALFREDO CAULIFLOWER CASSEROLE

PREP TIME: 30 MINS ⋯ COOK TIME: 1 HR — SERVES 3-4

INGREDIENTS

- 4 strips bacon
- 2 medium crowns broccoli, cut into bite-sized pieces
- 1 head cauliflower, cut into bite-sized pieces
- ¾ lb boneless skinless chicken breast, diced
- 2 Tbsp extra virgin olive oil
- 1 tsp salt
- 1 tsp black pepper
- 1 tsp Italian seasoning
- 3 Tbsp butter
- 2 Tbsp olive oil
- 6–10 cloves garlic, minced
- 1 Tbsp ground black pepper
- 8 oz heavy whipping cream
- 8 oz sour cream
- 2 cups mozzarella cheese, shredded
- 3/4 cup Italian cheese (parmesan, romano, etc), shredded

DIRECTIONS

1. Preheat oven to 350° F.
2. Cook bacon; dice when cooled. Set aside.
3. Add broccoli and cauliflower to a deep pot and set aside.
4. In a large skillet, sauté chicken in oil over medium heat. Add salt, pepper, and Italian seasoning when chicken is halfway cooked.
5. Finish cooking chicken, drain fat and set chicken aside.
6. Clean out skillet; melt butter over medium heat. Add olive oil, garlic, and black pepper and sauté for approx. 1 minute, then add whipping cream and sour cream.
7. Once mixture is warm, add cheese. Allow cheese to melt over the next 5 minutes (do not let the mixture bubble).
8. Add chicken and cooked bacon to pot with broccoli and cauliflower. Add hot cheese mixture and mix thoroughly.
9. Dump mixture into casserole dish and sprinkle with Italian seasoning.
10. Bake for approx. 45 minutes. If desired, cover the top with mozzarella cheese and broil for 3–5 minutes for a crunchy cheese crust. Watch closely! Don't burn!

> "I started on this diet because some people said it decreased their anxiety. So, you know, when you run your own business, there's a ton of anxiety. I said, 'I could do with a little less anxiety,' and I started on the diet. The weight loss is that wonderful side benefit!"

🌐 TONYSTARLIGHT.COM
🌐 TONYSTARLIGHTBIRDS.COM
ⓕ TSSHOWROOM
▶ TONYSTARLIGHTSHOWROOMPORTLANDOR

WATCH: LINKS.MMKCOOKBOOK.COM/TONY-OUTTAKES

KETO GARLIC TOAST
PREP TIME: 2 MINS · COOK TIME: 2 MINS · SERVES 4

INGREDIENTS

1½ Tbsp butter

1 egg

2 Tbsp almond flour

1 Tbsp coconut flour

½ tsp baking powder

½ tsp garlic salt

¼ tsp Italian seasoning

Pinch of salt

4 cloves garlic, minced

Parmesan cheese

DIRECTIONS

1. Preheat oven to broil.
2. Melt butter in a coffee mug (preferably a uniform cylinder).
3. In a small mixing bowl, whisk egg, almond flour, coconut flour, baking powder, garlic salt, Italian seasoning, and salt until fairly smooth (approx. 1 minute of whisking).
4. Pour mixture into mug with butter. Swirl and tap the mug on the counter until the mixture sits uniformly, getting rid of all the air pockets.
5. Microwave for 90 seconds.
6. Dump loaf out onto cutting board and slice into four pieces. Spread butter on each piece. Spread minced garlic over the butter, and then sprinkle Parmesan cheese on top.
7. Broil until golden brown. Careful! Don't burn!

- 🌐 SUSANNAHMARS.COM
- 🌐 MERIDETHKAYECLARK.COM
- 📷 CHEFJUANANDONLY

TOMATO SAUCE ⋯ CAN BE MADE IN ADVANCE

INGREDIENTS

1 cup garlic cloves

1 onion

1 bunch basil

109 oz can whole, peeled San Marzano tomatoes

6 oz tomato paste

1 cup white wine

1 cups water

⅛ cup oregano

⅛ cup salt

½ cup sugar

DIRECTIONS

1. Preheat oven to 400°.
2. Using a food processor, chop garlic, onion, and basil.
3. In a large, deep, oven-safe baking dish, add all sauce ingredients and stir until combined.
4. Bake for 1½ hours. Put through food mill and cool.

SUSANNAH MARS, MERIDETH KAYE CLARK, CHEF JUAN ZARAGOZA

We stepped into Chef Juan Zaragoza's elegant kitchen with two of Portland's biggest musical theater stars, Susannah Mars and Merideth Kaye Clark. Susannah has been called "the golden girl of the Northwest musical theatre scene," starring on stage, TV and film. Merideth is a multitalented multi-instrumentalist, with her most iconic role as Elphaba in the National Tour of *Wicked*. Chef Juan's classical-meets-the-unexpected technique puts this dish over the top!

CHICKEN PARMESAN

PREP TIME: 2 HRS ··· COOK TIME: 2 HRS   SERVES 4

INGREDIENTS

4 7 oz chicken breasts

4 cup panko bread crumbs

2 Tbsp Herbes de Provence

1 cup flour

6 eggs, beaten

1 cup canola oil

Tomato sauce (opposite page)

2 cups mozzarella cheese, shredded

¼ cup Parmesan cheese, grated

¼ bunch basil for garnish

DIRECTIONS

1. Preheat oven to 400° F.
2. Butterfly chicken breasts and pound out thin.
3. In a large bowl, mix panko with dry herbs.
4. Use the traditional breading technique: dip chicken in flour, then egg, then panko mix. Store until ready for use (can be done up to a day in advance).
5. In a large skillet, heat oil to 350° F (medium/medium-high heat).
6. Cook chicken on both sides until golden brown.
7. Drain on paper towel.
8. Arrange cooked chicken breasts on an ungreased baking sheet and cover with tomato sauce and cheese. Bake until cheese begins to brown.
9. Boil water in a large pot (to make sure pasta doesn't stick together, use at least 4 quarts of water for every pound of noodles). Add at least 1 Tbsp salt to water (the salty water adds flavor to pasta). Add pasta, stirring occasionally. Test pasta by tasting it. Drain pasta.
10. Portion spaghetti onto plate. Place chicken on top of spaghetti. Garnish with Parmesan and basil.

"I just tweaked it a little bit, changed the marinara and the breadcrumbs," says Chef Zaragoza. "Just doing it my way versus the old way."

Susannah and Merideth immediately burst into song—"He does it...his way!"

MARTI MENDENHALL ⋯ JAZZ SINGER, PODCASTER, AUTHOR

Margaritas have always been a personal favorite of mine. I love the unique blend of flavors and the hint of salt, and I don't need an excuse to drink one (and sometimes two)! I'm a bit more sophisticated now than I used to be, and I'm not very big on drinking all my dessert calories in one drink. It took me a long time to find out that there was something called sipping tequila, and an additional few years to discover Don Julio 70. This is a 100% blue agave tequila that has been double-filtered and is hands-down my absolute favorite! So let me save you some time. This recipe is my way to enjoy the margarita taste, watch my waistline and still savor the smooth, complex flavor of this delicious drink.

MARTI-RITA

PREP TIME: 3 MINS **SERVES 1**

INGREDIENTS

1 container common margarita salt

1 small lime

4 Ice cubes

1.5 oz of Don Julio 70® Añejo Claro Tequila (see pg. 50 for link) or other premium tequila

- MARTIMENDENHALL.COM
- MMKPODCAST.COM
- MARTI.MENDENHALL
- MARTIMENDENHALL

DIRECTIONS

1. Remove the lid from your margarita salt.
2. Squeeze the juice from one slice of lime into the lid.
3. Dip your glass (rocks glass is recommended) into the lime, then into the salt and rotate as necessary.
4. Shake off excess salt into the sink.
5. Add ice cubes.
6. Add one pinch of the margarita salt.
7. Add tequila.
8. Squeeze in the juice from ½ of the lime to taste.

Only 100 calories—Drink and enjoy!

BONUS TREATS

OREGON WINE PRESS CLASSIC MUSIC PAIRINGS
LINKS.MMKCOOKBOOK.COM/PAIRINGS

RUHLMAN'S RATIO APP
RUHLMAN.COM/APPS

OCHO RIOS® SCOTCH BONNET HOT SAUCE
LINKS.MMKCOOKBOOK.COM/HOT-SAUCE

KAJUN KETTLE FOODS CRAWFISH MONICA
KAJUNKETTLE.COM

BETTER THAN BOUILLON LOBSTER BASE
LINKS.MMKCOOKBOOK.COM/LOBSTER

DON JULIO® AÑEJO TEQUILA
LINKS.MMKCOOKBOOK.COM/TEQUILA

FRANGELICO
FRANGELICO.COM

NAPOLEON® OLIVE OIL
LINKS.MMKCOOKBOOK.COM/NAPOLEON

OLD BAY
LINKS.MMKCOOKBOOK.COM/OLDBAY

FIND MARTI'S MUSIC KITCHEN ONLINE

MMKPODCAST.COM
YOUTUBE.COM/MARTIMENDENHALL
PATREON.COM/MARTIMENDENHALL

IN PARTNERSHIP WITH OREGONMUSICNEWS.COM

MMK LIVE PERFORMANCES PLAYLIST
LINKS.MMKCOOKBOOK.COM/PERFORMANCES-S1

MMK PREVIEWS PLAYLIST
LINKS.MMKCOOKBOOK.COM/PREVIEWS-S1

"THE MORE I'M AWAY FROM YOU" BY MARTI MENDENHALL
LINKS.MMKCOOKBOOK.COM/THE-MORE-IM-AWAY-FROM-YOU

MMK ALL THE OUTTAKES
LINKS.MMKCOOKBOOK.COM/OUTTAKES

Made in the USA
Middletown, DE
13 November 2021